GW01417698

Creatures of

performance poems

Rosie Lugosi

purpleprosepress

Published by purpleprosepress 2003
5 Longford Road
Manchester M21 9WP
purpleprosepress@feline93.freeserve.co.uk

British Library Cataloguing-in-Publication Data
A catalogue record for this book is available from the British
Library

Printed by Walter Brown Printers
92 Newton Road, Lowton, Warrington WA3 1DG
E-mail: WalterBrown@wwmail.co.uk
Cover design by Alastair Fell
Cover author photos by David Burrows

Acknowledgements

Some of the poems have been read on the following TV and radio
stations and programmes: Granada Television (Granada Reports),
Channel 4 (Taste of the Vampire), BBC 1 (Flesh), BBC 4 (Dead Good
Poets Society), GMR and Woman's Hour.

Two Queens was first published in Mslexia – for Colin Watts
Callous Bi was written with Jo Warburton
With thanks to Fitz for the music.

ISBN 0 9536746 2 2

contents

V-A-M-P-I-R-E

What you got, baby I want it
What I need, I know you got it
All I'm asking is a little blood for me
(Just a little bite, just a little bite)

I'm about to rise from the grave
And all I'm asking is for you to be my slave
Give me a pintful when I fly home
(Just a little bite, just a little bite)

V-A-M-P-I-R-E, suck it from an artery
V-A-M-P-I-R-E, my fangs are sharpened specially
(Suck it from me, suck it from me)

Right now, it's imperative
That I get some Type O Negative
Tasting sweet as honey from your neck
(Just a little bite, just a little bite)

I'm gonna bite you all through the night
And all I'm asking is no sunlight
Get rid of the garlic and the holy water
(Just a little bite, just a little bite)

V-A-M-P-I-R-E, I love your carotid artery
V-A-M-P-I-R-E, be a blood donor for me
(Suck it from me, suck it from me)

callous bi

You were feeling rather tense
'Cos l was sitting on the fence
You were trying to take control
Of my indiscriminating role.

I couldn't help but hurt you
I couldn't help but make you cry
I couldn't help but hurt you
I'm just a callous bi.

You were feeling insecure
I might not shag you any more
But a greedy cow like me
Will fuck anyone that's free.

I couldn't help but hurt you
I couldn't help but make you cry
I couldn't help but hurt you
I'm just a callous bi.

You say that I should decide
I want my bread buttered both sides
But I want to swing both ways
I love guys and girls and gays.

I couldn't help but hurt you
I couldn't help but make you cry
I couldn't help but hurt you
I'm just a callous bi.

I made the horror films
(homage to John Cooper Clarke)

I made the horror films which never scared
Anyone, live or undead
Like Interview With The Bank Manager
And I Don't Give A Toss What You Did Last Summer.

They said Rosemary's Baby Bouncer was far too jolly
So was I Bought A Vampire Asda Trolley
Dracula Prince of Urmston got nowhere
Nor did Buffy the Born-Again Christian Slayer

No-one screamed at Night Of The Living Room
Or Creature From The Pink Lagoon
Silence Of The Mobile Phones went down the pan
Also The Wicker Basket Man

They laughed at The Satanic Kites Of Dracula
And the Texas Chainsaw Powertools Discount Price Massacre
I remade The Exorcist with the cast of The Bill
And Alien, starring Keith Harris and Orville

I should have known the public would hate her
When I cast Little Jimmy Krankie in the role of Terminator
Now I do costume drama. It's not going too well:
The Beeb have turned down my
Jane Austen's Nympho Biker Chicks From Hell.

Creatures of the Night

Roll up, roll up
Run up the stairs
Slam the door on car alarms
Breaking glass and breaking hearts,
Promises that no-one kept,
And conversations which pretend
That Friends and Frasier matter.
Pull up a chair, sit down
Make sure you're fastened in
Check your teeth are sharp,
Your hands and conscience nearly clean.

For
Here be tygers, here be dragons
Here be creatures of the night
With fiery eyes and painted faces
Grinning through their pearly whites
Curling round your ankles
Purring out their fairy tales and better than the real thing
Lies.

Watch us
Spinning stories out of air
Snap the sky into handbag mirror splinters
Raise the roof and use it as a parachute
Helter skelter down into the dark
Bring back nightmares cut into chainsaw
Hearts and red red roses
Oh, make mine marvellous!

Trade in
Their heaven and its rock of ages,
When to stand and when to kneel,

Its greatest hits on boxed CD
And find it in the yellow pages,
Its loyalty cards and five years' free credit
Its pink for spring and come on you reds
Its dye your hair though you know you're not worth it
Who to love and when to breed
And give another fiver to Children in Need.

Tonight, be
Cinderella in Versace torn in rags to wipe the floor
Confetti ripped up chewed up spat out
Mashed up flat out won't you be my wagon wheel,
Be Barbie with the head of Action Man
Be beautiful be ugly
Be the one that got away

Sing a song of sexiness
A pocket full of perversion
I'll sweep you off your feet
Or across my knee
Welcome to what you wished for
Trip the dark fantastic
Stick with me.

I'm being queer for Britain

I'm wearing black for Britain
So you can pack your wardrobes with BHS beige
Comfort yourselves in supermarket trainers
I'll take the strain in stilettos
Sweat it out in a rubber corset
So you can bask in polycotton
I'll camp it up and vamp it something rotten
Paint the town pitch so you can paint it
pastel flowers and frills
No one will stare
I'll wear black so you can fade into the walls.

I'm being queer for Britain
So you can sleep safe in your beds
Lullabyed to happy endings dreams
Of The Famous Five and Stars in their Eyes
It's great to be narrow and straight
To walk the streets and not get beaten up
By men in tight white t-shirts
Armed with God's own laws to tell them who to hate.

I'm being bent for Britain
So you boys can take the girlfriend home
To meet the folks
And never think twice about how many lies to spin
When mum and dad ask you what you did
and where you've been
I'll let you off the hook
You won't get called pouf
Or worry for a second that you'll lose your job
Because the boss hates a bloke who puts his knob
where he shouldn't

I'm being a lesbo for Britain
So you've got something to fill
Your sticky top-shelf entertainment
While you do it on Saturday nights
with the lights turned out
Thinking of England and flat on your back
Missionaries to a sexual suburban cul-de-sac
Be fruitful and multiply
While the Eye in the Sky says,
Normal art thou in my sight
You can walk up the aisle and be blessed
While you're dressed like a prat
In a penguin suit or avocado satin.

I don't do exactly what it says on the tin
Slaving away without a word of complaint
Still I battle through it
It's a hard job being queer for Britain,
But someone's got to do it.

why I wear black #1

It's the colour of bat's wings and graveyards
It makes me look sepulchral and grim
And it doesn't show bloodstains that would only come out
By repeatedly scrubbing with Vim.

It perfectly matches my coffin, my hair
It looks lovely in the moonlight
I'm glad that it hides the dust of the tomb
Because my laundrette closes at night.

I flirted with pink and with orange
Give me some credit for not wearing tack
Besides, it's the strongest sunblock in the world
...And that is why vampires wear black.

I get a kick out of you

I get a kick out of pain
Make me shiver and sweat oh!
Put on your stilettos
Trample me till I'm black and blue
And give me a kick with your shoe.

I don't want love that's mundane
I get no thrill ah!
From sex that's vanilla
You make my fantasies true
When I get a lashing from you.

I get a kick every time I'm kneeling there before you
I get a kick when you order me round
And tell me I don't deserve to adore you.

Treat me with regal disdain
Call me useless and bitch and make me scrub your kitchen
I'll satisfy - or else I hope you
Will give me a kicking or two.

Oh I get a kick
I get a kick
I get a flogging from you.

we have no bananas

Yes, we have no bananas.
We have no beliefs, no balls, no body, no backbone.
We can't believe it's not butter,
Though it's there in the small print
We just can't be bothered to read it.
We have no bloody idea.

We've lost the plot, lost our glasses
Our minds, our marbles,
The keys to our cars, our stairway to the stars.
It's all over bar the shouting.
We're lost in space.

We can't breathe, we can't sleep,
We can't pay the bills.
We can't hold it all together,
Can't buy good enough pills.

We're in the pink, we're in the red,
We're in it way over our heads.

We're marching to the beat of a different drummer,
We don't know what we did last summer
Even though we've seen the photos and the CCTV shots.
We've been framed.

We can't find the time, we can't find the door,
We can't remember what we came upstairs for.
We can't see the light, we can't keep up the fight
We can't tighten our belts, we can't meet Mr. Right.

We'd love a Babycham, we'd love to take you home with us,
We'd love Paris in the Spring

We'd love a Christmas bonus.
We've been told we are the champions and first past the post,
But we're up our own arses
Up against the wall
We can't keep up with the Joneses
We don't know jack.
We wouldn't know jig-a-jig if it jumped us in the dark.
We're a joke, a jerk-off.
We're all ordinary joes.
Bang bang, our baby shot us down.

Yes, we have no bananas.

safe sex message

Wanking is forever
It is all I need to please me
Sex toys stimulate and tease me
Things that buzz whirr and hum
Are all fun ways to come
Believe me…

Wanking is forever
Drop your knickers and caress it
Touch it stroke it and undress it
I can sleep sound all night
'Cos I've hit the spot right
Believe me…

I need self-love
What good's procrastination?
If you've got masturbation
Though life is hell
You can ring your own bell.

Wanking is forever
I just lick my little finger
Twirl it, make the moment linger
Because sex that's unsafe
Is not worth going to your grave for

Use latex gloves
And lube that's soft and silky
Wanking can fulfil me
Turn the switch to on
And I'll go all night long…

all kinds of everything

Moonlight and cemeteries
Things of the night
Zombies that eat your brains
Vampires that bite
Your funny phase of robbing graves
That 666 tattoo
All kinds of everything remind me of you.

Handcuffs and nipple clamps
Begging for more
You look so enticing
When you're down on all fours
Gagged and bound, there's not a sound
Though you're black and blue
All kinds of everything remind me of you.

The way you squeal
Six inch heels
Fishnet stockings too
Even a sex change could never change
The way I feel about you.

Hooks in the ceiling
A leash round your throat
That evening we spent sacrificing a goat
Leopardskin, absinthe and gin
The swish of bamboo
All kinds of everything remind me of you.

the Middle England tango

I'm from Cheshire, and it is my aspiration
To spread Middle England values through the nation
The South-East thinks it has it all
But what of Knutsford and Bramhall?
Where we dance to the Middle England Tango.

My children are called Hugo and Naomi
We'll be sending them to school in Cheadle Hulme
We've got a maths coach in every week
And Nanny's fluent in French and Greek
So they'll danser to the Middle England tango.

I drive a BMW for free
Paid by the company
I change it every June;
Then I've a four-wheel drive
It's for the morning school run
And for posing Sunday afternoon.

Once I bought all my food from Marks and Spencer
Now, though I hate the plebs who throng the Trafford Centre
The journey over Barton Bridge is
Worth the effort for Selfridges
Where I'll binge to the Middle England tango.

I buy my clothes on King Street from Armani
No I don't think it's barmy
Spending four grand on a dress;
I will pay through the nose
For shirts from Nicole Farhi
If I want to dress smartly
How can I pay any less?

At the weekend you'll not find me in Ikea
Like Canal Street it's been overrun with queers
John Lewis has by far
A better class of customer
To be a bigot to the Middle England tango.

can't take my eyes off you

It's just too good to be true
That I've met someone like you
Someone who comes out at night
And shrivels up in sunlight
Your skin flakes off and it's green
The crumbliest teeth ever seen
It's just too good to be true
Meeting a zombie like you.

The way you crawl out of your grave
Moaning as if you're in pain
Your eyes are hollow black pits
You rip your victims to bits
You bring home morsels to chew
An arm or a leg bone or two
Then you nibble my ear
Say the words I want to hear:

Let's go eat babies
Flavour in every bite
Yes pretty babies
Easy to digest just right
There are no maybes
Just take one mouthful and say
We'll start on babies
They are low-fat and lite
Then move to ladies
Because they taste just right
And let me eat you baby, let me eat you

You disinter the freshly dead
Your preference of course is the head
You suck out the brains with a straw

20

The smell just makes me love you more
Oh darling you've stolen my heart
And other vital body parts
Though I can't see a thing it is true
I can't take my eyes back off you.

Let's go eat babies
Flavour in every bite
Yes pretty babies
Easy to digest just right
There are no maybes
Just take one mouthful and say
We'll start on babies
They are low-fat and lite
Then move to ladies
Because they taste just right
And let me eat you baby, let me eat you…

my friend Gwen

My friend Gwen said say no to men
And smash the patriarchy on the way
Castration on demand – no we're not being silly
The only way for peace is to chop off their willies
We think men are vile
Don't agree? You're in denial
And maybe you should get some therapy
You can't call yourself a sister if you've got a mister
'Cos they're all the enemy.

My friend Jan said follow the clan
And don't wear a dildo or you may
Find that the sisters get judgemental and frowny
If you get into bondage then we'll drum you out the brownies
It's abusive and mental
I don't care if it's consensual
The very word alone oppresses me
I won't allow it, I don't want to talk about it
My mind's made up already.

succubus

She breathes on you; swear you don't feel a thing
But the looking-glass is misting
Damp with her condensation.
She writes: she 4 me, 4 eva, I love U, true
These are the ghosts she promises you.

Vinegar dreams that make you stand up
And suck your fingers
Chew the salt that crusts beneath your nails.
She fills you with silk, sandpaper,
Bites that tattoo your back and legs
with crescents of scarlet stars.

And she sings:
Baby baby, daddy shall have a new master
Swinging your heart on the end of a ribbon.
Sleepy yet?
Thumbs your eyelids till they
Sings in your ears until they
Pins your butterflies until they
Crouches on your ribs until they
Squeezes you until
Braids bits of 7-year-itch bitterness
Into the air that curls up from your tongue.

Writes: she 4 me, 4 eva, I love U, true
These are the ghosts she promised you.
She sings the blues
Purples you with a garden of rosy bruises
Small as her fists, wide as you can force it.
She is teeth and tongue and
Old enough to slip your window catches
The girl you never loved

But always looked for.
She never comes when you call. You cannot warm her.
She writes: she 4 me, 4 eva, I love U, true
These are the ghosts she promises you.

She sings black and blue murder
There's something she forgot to mention
If you could only speak her name
The one you keep forgetting.
She is no accident that just keeps happening.
She's the breath you gasp out,
She's your half-empty bed
The bottles rolling on the floor
Why you hate the weekends
Why it's just too hard to hold it all together
And why no other woman ever looks like her.
She 4 me, 4 eva, I love U, true
These are the ghosts she promised you.

two queens

I'd arranged the Palace Hotel bar, at seven. Figured
The cavernous hall, high gilded ceiling would suit
World-changers. They were already there;
Had ordered beer in straight glasses. I knew them at once:

Her, from the bas-reliefs in the Met; and her,
From technicolour gloss in A level History.
"You both look fatter," I said, "than the pictures."
"There's court portraitists for you," boomed Nefertiti,

Halfway through her pint. Patted a teak-stained
Roll of fat which hung about her navel. "Likewise:
When did you last see a royal virgin painted fat?"
Blared Elizabeth, and thumped me on the back. Clinked

Her glass with the serpent of old Nile, who hissed,
"I wasn't called the Beautiful-Woman-Is-Come
For nothing: whereas you, my dear... Look at us;
We are Beauty and the Bess!" They fell

Upon each other. The scourge of the Armada winked
Over the Egyptian's shoulder. "It's handbags
At dawn for us," she cackled through brown teeth. Continued
Later: "We're going. Somewhere with a lower ceiling.

Dancing. And tobacco." I pointed them the hundred yards
Towards Canal Street. They wove across the pavement,
Adjusting their wigs. I stole their beerglasses, have them still.
Can see their fingersmears and lipmarks on the rim.

a pervert like you

When you speak without permission
When everything you do is wrong
When you beg me to treat you badly
It gives me strength to carry on.

The world may never know the reason why
I treat you like I do:
It's 'cos you're a pervert
Through and through.

You put on your stockings and suspenders
You shave your chest and then your chin
Your only prayer and consolation
Is that I'll let you kiss my ring.

The world may never know the reason why
I flog you black and blue:
It's 'cos you're a pervert
Through and through.

Being a bitch queen isn't easy
I have to practice long and hard
I get my hope and inspiration
Reading the Marquis de Sade.

The world may never know the reason why
I love you like I do:
It's 'cos you're a pervert
Through and through;
The world may never know the reason why
I love you like I do:
It's 'cos you're a pervert
And I am one too.

why I wear black #2

Because grey makes me look like
the stuff I fish out of the vacuum cleaner.
Because brown makes me look like shit.
Because red makes me look like nosebleeds.
Because blue makes me look like bruises.
Because yellow makes the bruises look like they're fading.
They're still an ache.
Because pink is healing scars.
Because green is knuckled fists.
Because white is the broken teeth of hurled plates.
Because purple is back to bruises,
The ones that bloom around the eye.
I say, I walked into a door.
Because no-one else is there.
Because it's a clean slate.

everytime you say goodbye

Everytime you say goodbye
I cry with laughter
I can take that noose I made
Down from the rafters
I've been plotting murder
Dear God, you had to go
Death seemed the only answer
Then you said that magical word.

Everytime you say goodbye
I smile to heaven
I can put the safety on
My AK47
I think so little of you
I planned for you to go
I bought you such good life insurance
It was illogical to say no.

Everytime you say goodbye
The words are so elating
I don't need that six foot hole
That I've been excavating
There's no thing finer
Than you saying you're going to Asia Minor
I'm so glad you said goodbye.